I0616167

LIVING A TRANSFORMED LIFE

LIVING A
TRANSFORMED LIFE

ASHTON REMOLE

Contents

Introduction

I have been a Christian for as long as I can remember, but I didn't really start taking it seriously until high school. In my youth I read my Bible, my playlist was primarily worship music, and my family was at church every Sunday, but despite all those "good things" I didn't understand how real God is. I went to a homeschool co-op group called Illumination for my second through twelfth grade school years. In the high school program, there was a Bible curriculum that covered all the different world religions. I looked at the different religions and dove into them in detail. During this, I began to doubt everything I knew about the Lord. I wasn't sure He was real. Was everything I had known and experienced before false? Was there really a God who loved me unconditionally? After weeks of doubt, I lived a week acting as if I didn't believe in the Lord. I wrestled with serious doubt, and boy was that a rough week. I had never experienced the emptiness I felt that week. I lacked self control and was struggling with anxiety and depression. At the end of the week, I went to the Lord sobbing. I told Him that I was sorry for doubting Him and that I believe in Him and I know that He is who He says He is. I was overwhelmed with His peace and His love for me. This was when I really knew I believed in the Lord on my own without the influence of my parents, teachers, friends, or leaders. Since then, the Lord has walked me through some hard things like anxiety to the point of panic attacks, depression to the point of struggling with thoughts of suicide, and I am still here to testify of His goodness, faithfulness, and never-ending strength in our weakness. God is good! He is here for you! I want to share what the Lord has walked me through with you, and how you can grow in your relationship with Christ.

As believers, we must allow the Lord to transform every part of our lives. The Word says we must not be like the world, but be transformed by the renewing of our minds (Romans 12:2). My hope and prayer for this book is that you learn how the Lord can move in your life, how to read the Word and spend time with your Father, how to handle common struggles in the faith, and how to truly trust in the Lord. I pray for breakthrough and renewal over your life in Jesus' name!

The Secret Place

A Quiet Time vs. The Secret Place

"H*e who dwells in the secret place of the Most High*
Shall abide under the shadow of the Almighty.
I will say of the Lord, 'He is my refuge and my fortress;
My God, in Him I will trust.'"
Psalm 91:1-2 NKJV

Secret: hiding place, privately, protection
Dwells: to stay for a time; to live as a resident

Growing up in a Christian household and attending a Christian co-op, this chapter in Psalms was read often. I could quote these verses without thinking twice, but it wasn't until after I graduated college that I began to really understand what these verses truly meant.

All throughout middle and high school I had "quiet times" on a regular basis, but I never actually dwelled in the secret place. I never understood the difference until the Lord began to show me what that truly means. My quiet times sometimes took place in my bedroom, some in the kitchen of my home, and some at various coffee shops. I read the next chapter of scripture that I was going through at the time, took notes on things that stood out, and would often pray. Though this was great, and I was moving in the right direction, God showed me He is so much more than a routine that I can do anywhere.

Let's take a look at the definitions above in the original context. Look at the definition of secret in this verse's context. Hiding place and privately really jump out because that means we are to be ALONE with the Lord. This does not mean you can't do Bible studies at a coffee shop or with friends and family, but the Lord calls us to be alone with Him. Scripture says, "go into your room, and when you have shut your door, pray to your Father who is in the secret place..." (Matthew 6:6, NKJV). He wants us to have one-on-one time so we can truly know Him and hear from Him without distractions. When we want to grow closer to someone it requires us having time with just that person to truly get to know them for who they are. The Lord already knows us, but wants us to come to Him so He can reveal more about Himself to us in an intimate way.

Being in the secret place means to truly and consistently pray privately, read the Word of the Lord, worship the Father, and sit with God regularly. He wants to teach you and speak to you, but it requires you to be consistently still with Him. One day of school doesn't do much good for a student, but consistently going back to school helps the student learn and grow in passion and maturity for the subjects.

The definition for dwell that particularly stands out is "to live as a resident." Just as you keep returning to your home after school or work, keep returning to intimately being with your Father. God is our home. Sitting with the Lord and worshipping Him in this way can't be done while you are in the middle of a coffee shop. God desires our whole heart, our sincere worship, our deepest questions and requests, and every emotion we may feel to be brought to His feet. Jesus said, "My yoke is easy and My burden is light" (Matthew 11:30, NKJV). He wants to walk us through every need, hurt, desire, or thought we are facing. We have to be willing to make time for the Father if we want an intimate relationship with Him.

Quiet times are good and help us know the Word more, but we are called to be in the secret place with the Father and that helps us to know Him, His heart, and His will.

How to Pray

"*In this manner, therefore, pray:*
Our Father in heaven,
Hallowed be Your name.
Your kingdom come.
Your will be done
On earth as it is in heaven.
Give us this day our daily bread.
And forgive us our debts,
As we forgive our debtors.
And do not lead us into temptation,
But deliver us from the evil one.
For Yours is the kingdom and the power and the glory forever. Amen."
Matthew 6:9-13 NKJV

Format: Praise, Forgiveness, Request

"*In this manner, therefore, pray: Our Father in heaven, Hallowed be Your name. Your kingdom come. Your will be done On earth as it is in heaven...*"
I have been praying since I was a little girl. Every night, my parents would help me pray a simple prayer to help me build the habit of praying and understand that we can talk to our Heavenly Father. I can't remember the exact moment I learned about the passage above, but I have known it for as long as I can remember. Despite that, I never understood that this was the perfect example of prayer until years later. Jesus tells us that this is how we should pray. He not only begins by

giving praise to the Father, but half of His prayer is praise. There is always something we can praise the Lord for. It is impossible to run out of praise for the One who is the Creator of all and is good, pleasing, and perfect in every way. He is more than deserving of our worship; and worship should never be neglected or come second to making our requests.

"...Give us this day our daily bread. And forgive us our debts, As we forgive our debtors..." Jesus continues by asking for forgiveness (Jesus was and is perfect. He didn't need forgiveness, but showed us this as an example). After giving praise to the Father, ask Him to forgive you of anything you know you have fallen short in and ask Him to reveal to you anything you may be doing in your heart or in action that is displeasing to Him. Asking the Lord to reveal areas you are falling short on can be really hard. I know I wrestled with it before actually asking for that kind of revelation. I didn't know if I wanted to give up something I didn't even intend to be dishonoring to God. I was scared of how much God would say I needed to fix. There was my problem. It was never about me, to begin with. It was always about Him and His purpose and plan for my life. My life is not my own, it is His and has always been His. I needed to let go of my pride and humble myself at the feet of Jesus to let Him transform me through prayer. So yes, ask for forgiveness of things you know you did wrong, but also ask for the Lord to search your heart in its deepest corners to bring to light any darkness that may be residing there.

"...And do not lead us into temptation, But deliver us from the evil one. For Yours is the kingdom and the power and the glory forever. Amen." Jesus then says to make our requests known to the Lord. This is when we ask for the things we need or want from the Lord. Psalm 37:4-5 says, "Delight yourself also in the Lord, And He shall give you the desires of your heart. Commit your way to the Lord, Trust also in Him, and He shall bring it to pass" (NKJV). The Father can give us the desires of our heart if we delight in Him; because if we are close to Him, our de-

sires and His desires for us will begin to align. God is your Father. He is your Dad. Think of Him as the sweetest, kindest, and most loving Father you can imagine. He is even more than that. He wants to hear your every question, hurt, request, and desire. He wants to be there for you like a father. Rest in your Father's arms and lay everything at His feet. He is wise and knows what is best for you. Trust His perfect will, knowing that we may not understand every "why," but He does and He will use it for our benefit and His glory (Romans 8:28).

Something my parents and a very sweet friend and mentor of mine taught me is that prayer is our communication with God. It is a conversation, and a conversation goes two ways. Imagine you are at work or school, and someone walks up to you, says "You're cool", asks you for a favor, and then walks away without giving you a chance to respond to anything. You wouldn't consider this a conversation. All they did was say something to you and didn't let you respond. How often do we do this to the Lord? We go to Him, praise Him, ask Him for things, and move on with our day. Do we actually give God space to speak to us? After you make your requests known to the Father, ask Him to give you ears to hear His voice and not be confused with your own thoughts, then sit alone in silence with the Lord and wait for Him to speak (Psalms 5:3 in NLT says "wait expectantly"). His voice is always filled with peace. God is not the author of confusion. So, if you hear mixed messages, it is your flesh or the enemy trying to distract you from hearing God's voice or make you second guess what your Father said. Continue to seek the Lord's voice until you have clarity and peace about what you have heard. The more you listen to Him speak, the easier it becomes to discern His voice (John 10:27). God can also speak through His Word, through music, and through others. God is over all things and can choose how He speaks to His children, but always be sure to make space for Him in your time in the secret place to hear from Him. Don't leave until you have allowed room for Him to speak.

In Matthew 6:6, we also see that prayer is to be done in private. Meaning, that you are called to have further intimacy with the Lord and that your prayer life isn't something to boast about. Prayer isn't about sounding good or performing well to the people around you. It is about growing a deeper relationship with the Father. Jesus also is an example of going away in private to pray, as He does this several times during His earthly ministry.

Pray by offering praise to the only One deserving of it, ask Him to forgive you, make your requests known to Him, and make space for the Lord to reply.

Heart Song

"I will sing to the Lord as long as I live;
I will sing praise to my God while I have my being."
Psalms 104:33 NKJV

Worship is something so near and dear to my heart. I love to sing, play instruments, and just sit with the Father. I grew up singing and began guitar lessons in late middle school. I started to fall in love with music even more and was a worship leader in my church. The Lord provided so much growth in my understanding of worship during this season and I am so grateful for the clarity He provided.

Specifically, I want to talk about private worship. Yes, it is so sweet and precious to have a community to worship with corporately. I would greatly encourage you to attend corporate worship on a regular basis, as this is biblical (Hebrews 10:25). However, every part of our lives should be done for the Lord as an act of worship (Colossians 3:23-24, Hebrews 13:15-16). The Lord desires our worship and surrender to Him. He created us to worship.

I believe that private worship to the Lord is a crucial and transformative part of our time in the secret place. Worship can look different for everyone and you don't have to be musically inclined to worship. We are to make a joyful noise to the Lord and sing songs of praise to Him (Psalms 100:1-2). He doesn't need it to sound like the person you hear on the radio; your worship is beautiful to your Father no matter what it sounds like. He wants to hear your voice sing to Him.

In my time in the secret place, I often play soaking music and sing whatever my heart is grateful for and anything that comes to mind about the Lord's greatness. Soaking music is simply Christian instrumental music that is often used for times of prayer and worship, which is why it is so perfect for the secret place. Sing your heart's song to the Lord. What are you grateful for? How have you seen the Lord move in your life or in the lives of others? How has the Lord revealed His majesty, sovereignty, greatness, magnitude, kindness, love, mercy, joy, strength, peace, or wisdom? Sing about Him to Him. Sing your heart's cry of praise and adoration to your Father who loves you. If this feels too uncomfortable to you at first, you can pick a few worship songs to play from your device and worship in that way. Simply begin taking baby steps to further your intimacy with your Heavenly Father.

Singing our heart songs to the Lord brings us to a place of humility and surrender. It allows our hearts to be more sensitive to the Spirit so that He can move in our lives and we can be transformed into the person God created us to be. Our mindset shifts from our needs and wants to praise. We shift our focus to gratitude for who He is and what He has done. The Word says we are transformed by the renewing of our minds (Romans 12:2). Spend intentional time in worship of the Father, allowing Him to move by His Spirit in us so that we can be transformed. This allows us to keep a heart posture of humility before Him and surrender to His will.

How to Read the Word

"*So then faith comes by hearing, and hearing by the word of God*"
    Romans 10:17 NKJV

Scripture study is such a large topic with a variety of different perspectives and patterns of how it should be done. I want to show you how I study scripture in a way that is practical and isn't overloaded with steps. Studying the Word can be as complicated as you want to make it. If you love deep elaborate studies then just dive even deeper into some of the rich history and definitions. If you like to keep things simple, you don't have to do that every time you get into the secret place. There is a balance and you will need to find your own rhythm of how the Lord wants you to study His Word in a way that helps you grow in understanding, knowledge, and love for Him.

Before I begin reading, I ask the Lord to reveal Himself to me in His Word. I ask Him to show me anything He wants me to gain out of the study. I ask for clarity and understanding of His Word. Now, I am definitely not perfect at this. There are times I just began reading and didn't ask for guidance before starting. However, I do find it helps me have a more productive and fruitful study of His Word when I ask Him to help me study it.

If you are a new believer or someone who is trying to better understand the basics of Christianity, I recommend starting with one of the Gospels at the beginning of the New Testament (Matthew, Mark, Luke, and John). I would specifically recommend John or Matthew. The Gospels share the life of Jesus on earth and His ministry. He reveals His purpose for coming to earth and shares many teachings that are applicable to us as His followers. However, all of the Bible is meant to be read, studied, and is available for anyone willing to learn from it. If you feel the Lord is wanting you to read a particular passage, chapter, or book of the Bible, start there! In my experience, I know it is from the Lord if I can't get it off my mind and I have peace about starting there. I typically do one book at a time, but sometimes I will go through multiple books at once. As I am writing this, I am reading through Isaiah and Psalms.

My time in the secret place usually goes something like this... **Prayer to help me study well, read the chapter for that day, take notes and look up definitions, prayer session, and worship session.** Yours may have a completely different layout, but I found that making sure I hit all of these points has greatly boosted my understanding and love for Him and His Word.

As you read, I recommend highlighting anything that stands out to you. Within those highlights, I like to underline the main point that stands out. From that, you can look up definitions of keywords using Blue Letter Bible or Strong's Concordance. Those are helpful resources to give the proper definition of that word in a historical context. In some of the devotions in this book, you may notice some words with definitions listed from the verse for that day. Those definitions were gained from the use of those resources to help you better understand what that verse is talking about.

After reading and pulling definitions, I take notes on what the Lord showed me through the passage I was reading. You can use a notebook or write in your Bible. I do a bit of both. I like to have room to write more in my notebook, but I enjoy flipping through my Bible and seeing how the Lord spoke to me in that passage with the brief takeaways I have written down.

Allow the Word of God to transform you and the way you live. You don't need to overcomplicate it. Just spend time with the Father in His Word and He will help you grow in understanding. Everyone starts somewhere, but it is time to just get started! Not feeling confident in knowing how is not an excuse. You will never know how unless you just start. If you have already started and it's a habit for you, keep going. Don't quit! Keep growing and don't be content with where you are. Always try to know more and love more. The Word talks about how we must move on to solid food and should not remain on baby's milk (Hebrews 5:13-14). The wisdom of God never runs out and there is always more for us to grow in.

On Fire

Constant Pursuit

"*B*ut seek first the kingdom of God and His righteousness,
and all these things shall be added to you."
Matthew 6:33 NKJV

I am sure you saw the topic for this section, which is called, "On Fire." You may be wondering what that means... Let me explain it to you the way the Lord has shown me. When I see someone who is on fire for God, they are knowledgeable of His Word, are showing the fruit of the Spirit, living unashamed of the gospel, and consistently spending time in the secret place. They live in constant pursuit of the Lord. Everything they do is in effort to bring them closer to the Father.

Our walk with Jesus isn't something we can do halfheartedly. Let's say we want to become extremely athletic. We want to become a runner and build muscle, but we only go to the gym two times a week and don't eat a healthy diet. We won't see much progress with that little effort. However, if we begin to eat healthy and workout consistently we can see growth. Why? Because we shifted our focus to our long-term goal and our habits followed suit with the lifestyle we are pursuing. The same applies with becoming someone who is on fire for God. If we shift our focus to pursuing Him–seeking first the kingdom of God–there will be a transformation in our lives (Matthew 6:33). We will become on fire for Him because we are keeping our eyes fixed on Him.

Living in constant pursuit means to keep putting God first in our daily lives. He can never be second place to something, if we want to be on fire. So, shift your eyes to the Lord. Seek Him with your whole heart. Be transformed by the renewing of your minds (Romans 12:2).

Consistency in the Secret Place

"But they delight in the law of the Lord,
meditating on it day and night."
Psalms 1:2 NLT

Now that we know what the secret place is, it is time to talk about consistency. Oftentimes in the workout community, we see people talk about how consistency is more important than perfection. Even if we have a bad workout or run out of time to finish what we planned, doing what we can is better than skipping a day. We still did something and that is progress.

The same idea can apply to spending time with the Lord. If you are having a hard time hearing from the Lord, still sit with Him and listen. If you only have ten minutes, spend every second being with the Father. If you are out of town and forgot to bring your note-taking supplies, take notes on your device and write them in when you get home. There is absolutely no excuse to neglect consistent time with the Lord. If you feel you don't have time, then make time. The Lord is more important than any other thing in our lives and cannot be second to anything. Don't wait until an extra hour appears in your schedule. It will never come. If you can't do anything else, listen to the Word on your phone while driving to work or school. Play worship music in your car and sit with the Lord. The Lord understands your circumstances and will meet you where you are, but you need to be willing to put in the consistent effort to meet with Him daily.

Psalms tells us that we should meditate on the Word day and night–meaning all the time (Psalms 1:2). We should never remove our focus from the Lord. He is always our top priority. I had to come to the point of realizing that "I ran out of time," "there isn't enough time in the day," or "I was really busy this week" are never, under any circumstances, an excuse to miss time with the Lord. You will make time for things you find important. Being in the secret place is more important than anything else, and if we want to be on fire for the Lord then we have to make time to be with Him. It is better for you to neglect sleep than to miss out on knowing your Father. Matthew 16:24 says, "Then Jesus told his disciples, 'If anyone would come after me, let him deny himself and take up his cross and follow me'" (ESV).

Abiding

"R*emain in Me, and I will remain in you.*
For a branch cannot produce fruit if it is severed from the vine,
and you cannot be fruitful unless you remain in me."
John 15:4 NLT

Remain: other translations (such as NKJV) use the word abide
Abide: to be vitally connected to

We live in a busy world that has a mindset and expectation of running nonstop. There is a lack of rest in society. Jesus told us to go to Him to find rest (Matthew 11:28). As long as we are with Him, it doesn't matter our circumstances, we can have rest and exhibit the fruit of peace. However, we can't bear fruit if we aren't attached to the vine.

Let's say there is an apple tree. The apples will grow to be delicious and ripe as long as the branch is attached to the tree. If the branch is broken off, the apple will die and no longer be of use to the farmer. Even if the branch is taped back to the tree, it will still die because touching it isn't being connected with it. You can't live a fruitful life apart from God. You can't just be near Him (just going to church or reading the Word occasionally), you must abide or remain IN Him.

Abiding also goes with trust. We can know we are abiding in Him if we are reliant on Him in every situation. Issues at work? Abide in Him and trust He will sustain you. Issues with your relationships? Abide in Him and know He will never leave you nor forsake you (Hebrews 13:5). Struggling to find your path and know what your future holds? Abide in Him and know He has a plan for you and His ways are good, pleasing, and perfect (Romans 12:2). God alone knows the future and every detail about you. He knows exactly what you need and when you need it. He is your sustainer. To produce good fruit (Galatians 5:22) and be on fire for God, you must rest in the Source of life.

You should always desire to be in the presence of God. Remain there with your Dad. The more we remain with Him, the more we can be like Him. Paul also says in 1 Corinthians 11:1, "And you should imitate me, just as I imitate Christ..." (NLT). Make every effort to be like your Father. Walk more like Jesus in the way we love, serve, and act. The best way to know His character is to abide in Him. He will show you His character and be your source of strength, love, and life. Rest in your Heavenly Father and know He has you in His arms and will sustain you in all things. As you rest in Him, allow Him to transform you into a fruitful child of the King.

Consistency in Prayer

"*A lways be joyful. Never stop praying.*
Be thankful in all circumstances,
for this is God's will for you who belong to Christ Jesus."
1 Thessalonians 5:16-18 NLT

Think about any relationship... friendship, dating, or marriage. How well do those thrive without communication? Especially my fellow married friends... How well does your day-to-day go when there is a lack of communication? Things can get interesting really quickly–and not in a good way. There are often misunderstandings, which lead to arguments and bitterness. Clear and constant communication is vital to a healthy relationship. It establishes trust and helps us to know each other better. How much more important do you think it is to have constant and clear communication with the Father?

We already know that prayer is how we communicate thoughts of gratitude and praise to the Lord as well as making our request known to Him. We also know that during our time of prayer we hear from the Lord; and that the more we listen, the easier it is to discern His voice (John 10:27). His Word commands that we "never stop praying." It is not a suggestion. God wants to be in constant communication with His children. This allows us to better understand the workings of our Father and His will for us. It also helps us to be open with the Lord about every detail of our lives. If we only go to the Lord with big things, then how personal are we letting our relationship be with our Creator? Allow the Lord to be in every detail of our lives by being constantly in prayer.

We won't be close to someone we hardly speak to. To be on fire for God, we must be close to Him. To be close to Him, we must communicate with Him. To communicate with Him, we must consistently pray. Pray while you work, cook, drive, or workout. Allow the Lord to hear from you–that is His desire. The Lord will transform you when you let yourself be consistently communicating with Him. Allow Him to increase your fire for Him through prayer.

Sold Out

"So never be ashamed to tell others about our Lord.
And don't be ashamed of me, either, even though I'm
in prison for Him. With the strength God gives you,
be ready to suffer with me for the sake of the Good News."
2 Timothy 1:8 NLT

As a kid, I remember singing, "This Little Light of Mine" at my VBS. The lyrics talk about not hiding our light under a bushel, but to let our light for Jesus shine to the world. The lyrics of this simple children's song still rings true as mature believers. We cannot be afraid to shine for Jesus. If we are allowing God to transform us by renewing our minds, then we must be willing to live transformed lives, not just have an experience (Romans 12:2).

Matthew 28:18-20 is the Great Commission that Jesus gave His disciples. The Great Commission is our calling, it wasn't just for the eleven—this is, going and making disciples. How can we shine the light of Jesus and make new disciples, if we are hiding the fact that we are Christians? You cannot be ashamed to share the gospel and how it has transformed you (your testimony) to others. Living on fire means living sold out and unashamed of Him. Matthew 10:32-33 says, "Everyone who acknowledges me publicly here on earth, I will also acknowledge before my Father in heaven. But everyone who denies me here on earth, I will also deny before my Father in heaven" (NLT). I don't know about you, but I do not want to be denied on judgment day.

Furthermore, why wouldn't I want to share about the One who completely transformed my life?

Never be afraid to share your faith. Living on fire also means to be bold. We can't be afraid of the world's judgment. They judge people who aren't believers, how much more so will they judge those who disagree with their worldview (John 15:18-19, John 17:14)? We belong to Christ and not the world so our approval only needs to come from Him. Therefore, live completely and totally sold out for Him. Live with the purpose of making Him known. It doesn't matter who sees you, but only that your Father knows your heart for Him—a heart that is unashamed and in love.

Be bold and love the Father and others so deeply you are willing to risk your appearance and reputation for the sake of their eternity. What kind of love knows the saving grace, but refuses to share it for self-preservation? It's not about you. It's not about me. It's about Jesus. Live your life for Jesus, because it's all His. We have the privilege to be a vessel for His purpose. Don't forget that it is a privilege.

Got that Jesus Glow

"When you produce much fruit, you are my true disciples.
This brings great glory to my Father."
John 15:8 NLT

*"But the Holy Spirit produces this kind of fruit in our lives:
love, joy, peace, patience, kindness, goodness, faithfulness,
gentleness, and self-control. There is no law against these things!"*
Galatians 5:22-23 NLT

Have you ever met someone and you just knew they had to be a genuine believer? I definitely have. That is actually biblical. Matthew 7:15-20 talks about how you will know if people are true followers of Jesus by the fruit in their lives. The fruit we are talking about is the fruit of the Spirit from Galatians 5:22-23. You can tell if someone is truly following the Lord by the fruit in their lives–that is, by the way they act. What kind of fruit are you producing? Just like a bad tree will produce bad fruit, so will people if they are not connected to the True Vine.

When we abide in Christ, we WILL produce fruit (John 15). If there is a lack of fruit in your lives, check your heart and your habits. Are you truly abiding in the Vine? If not, allow the Lord to transform your lifestyle to the one He wants you to live. Allow the Gardener to tend the soil of your soul so you can grow. Your friends, Christians or not, will know if you are bearing fruit. Your non-christian friends will notice you pulling away from worldly tendencies (John 17:14). They will notice a lifestyle shift that makes you less like the world. This is amazing and desirable, because, as we have mentioned, our goal is to please God, not the world. Your Christian friends will notice a spark inside you. A fire being lit by your Father to be more like Him. In other words, "you got that Jesus glow." You will glow from the inside out with the light of Christ, because you, have changed for the better through the workings of the Holy Spirit. Praise the Lord for this amazing gift of transformation!

Glowing for the Lord is also an amazing way to reach the lost and reflect a life that is on fire for God. People notice a life that is different, a kind of love that is unconditional and genuine (even though you may not know them well), a joy that is uncontainable, a peace in hard circumstances, and a kindness to the undeserving. These qualities turn the heads of unbelievers, because no one else will act this way. By being different for the sake of Christ, we are planting seeds for the lost. Our nature is self-preserving, but God's love is for others. Allow the Lord to give you that Jesus glow and live on fire for His kingdom.

Relationships

Our Number One

"Do not make idols or set up caved images, or sacred pillars,
or sculptured stones in your land so you may worship them.
I am the Lord your God."
Leviticus 26:1 NLT

Idol: a representation or symbol of a false god, a person or thing that is greatly admired, loved, or revered

When we read through scripture (especially in the Old Testament), we see time and time again the worship of false gods. Today, we still see false gods and idols, such as Buddha, crafted from gold and sitting in a person's home, business, or place of worship. More than likely, if you are reading this, you are a Christian and probably aren't actively worshiping things like Buddha. However, you still may have idols in your life that you are unaware of.

Within the Christian community, believers strive to worship the Lord alone. This is amazing, but it also means the enemy often works in subtle ways—using even good things—to cause God's children to stumble. Idols I frequently see in the Church are phones, social media, body image, video games, books, friendships, boyfriends, girlfriends, spouses, hobbies, and money. Yes, this is a long list and yes, there are still many more that could be listed. If we are checking our messages or talking to significant others or friends so much that we neglect to spend time with our Heavenly Father (or reduce the time we ought to spend) then we have made that an idol. We are saying that those things are more important than God.

An idol is something that we worship. We are intentionally designed to worship, so if we don't worship our Creator, we will worship something else. Something is always going to be first in our lives, and we have to be willing to consistently make God first. Nothing can come before Him, nothing is greater than Him, and nothing is deserving of eternal praise, but Him.

When I first got married, it was so easy for me to make my husband my first priority. I wanted to pack his lunch, see him out the door for work, cook him dinner, make sure the house was spotless, and then do anything else I needed to do. On days we were both off work, we would hang out all day long from the time we arose to bedtime. The Lord convicted me of worshiping the gift instead of the Giver. I was idolizing my husband over the One who gave him to me. I had to reevaluate my heart and routines and make changes to keep the Lord as my number one and my husband number two. I could still do all those things for my husband, but I needed to make sure I was still prioritizing time in the secret place before doing all those things.

In relationships of any kind, it is a give-and-take. We have to pour into relationships. Scripture teaches that we can only love because He first loved us. If we want to be more loving and be able to pour continually into our relationships, then we must prioritize the Source of love before the ones we are pouring into. If we do not, we will run dry–because we separate ourselves from our Sustainer. Your Father must always be your number one. He is not second to anything or anyone. There would be nothing without Him, so worship the Creator, not the created.

God is Enough

" The Lord is merciful and compassionate,
  slow to get angry and filled with unfailing love."
Psalms 145:8 NLT

I remember a time in my life when I was so eager to be in a relationship. I liked a guy (now my husband) and I couldn't wait for him to ask me out. I had never dated anyone else or truly liked anyone in that manner before. I remember feeling so ready for the season of singleness to be over. It wasn't until I stopped obsessing over being asked out, that it finally happened. I believe the Lord knew exactly what He was doing when He allowed it to happen this way.

During my season of singleness, I was still communing with the Lord. I didn't know what the secret place was yet (so if you're single, you're a step ahead), but I was having quiet times and praying frequently. However, I was not living surrendered to His timing. I would say, "It'll happen in His timing," but truly believing that was different. I wondered if this guy, whom I felt the Lord told me would be my husband, would ever ask me out. I know it's easy to think it will never happen for you, or that maybe you misread signals of mutual interest in one another. You may even think God has forgotten about you. This is simply not the case. Everything God does is intentional.

Toward the end of my time as a "single pringle," I learned to truly let go of the timing I wanted and trust that the Lord had it under control. To truly believe this statement I kept telling myself, "It'll happen in His timing." I changed my focus to more of God. I had something I wanted to fill in my heart. God is enough to fill that void in your heart. You don't need a boyfriend or girlfriend to fill that place. Actually, you will find, they eventually won't satisfy the void in your heart once the newness wears off. If you want a lasting relationship, God has to be your number one. Yes, boyfriends, girlfriends, husbands, or wives are all so wonderful and such incredible blessings from your Father in heaven. They are not a necessity or substitute for God. You can't try to fill a void with human connection that only God was meant to fill. He is enough. He is your sustainer. He is the only one who can love you endlessly, without fail. Humans will fail you at some point or another, because we are imperfect people. God never will.

Maybe you're still in your season of singleness. If so, let this time be for growing and strengthening your relationship with Christ. Learn to let your Father fill every space in your heart. You will be stronger and better prepared for your partner. I like to think of godly relationships like a triangle. You and the person you will be with one day are the bottom two corners and God is the top corner. If you and the other person meet at the bottom of the triangle, God is not present in your relationship and you become further from God in the process. If you meet at the top, God is in your relationship and you both have to chase after God to find each other. So keep chasing your Sustainer and the only One who can love for all eternity. It will happen in His timing.

A Call to Purity

*"Let there be no sexual immorality, impurity, or greed among you.
Such sins have no place among God's people."*
Ephesians 5:3 NLT

*"for God bought you with a high price. So you must honor
God with your body."*
1 Corinthians 6:20 NLT

Dating someone is so beautiful and sweet. The excitement can be overwhelming and it is easy to be ready for the next step in your relationship. We hugged, then we held hands, then he kissed my hand, and then he kissed my cheek. A line has to be drawn somewhere in order to remain pure. It is easy to want the next thing before you should take that next step. It is easy to desire taking the next step, so much so, you lose sight of your boundaries. This is how people make mistakes and go too far.

When you are dating, it is so important to have strict boundaries to keep you from falling into impurity. If you do something that makes you want more than you should, or your mind begins to drift there, then you've gone too far. Make strict rules and hold each other accountable. Do not allow your flesh to get caught up in something that grieves the Holy Spirit. Be open and vulnerable with the person you are dating and tell them when that kiss or touch was too intimate for you. There may not be anything sinful about what was done, but the act could lead to sinful thoughts of lust. There is no shame in honesty and certainly not in purity.

Allow yourself to be open and honest with each other so that your relationship can be pure and pleasing to the Lord. You can also be an example of a godly relationship to the people around you. You will look different to the world and that is good. Be a light in the darkness by being pure and Christlike in your relationship.

Committed

"And he said, 'This explains why a man leaves his father and mother and is joined to his wife, and the two are united into one.' Since they are no longer two but one, let no one split apart what God has joined together."
Matthew 19:5-6 NLT

Marriage is a covenant between a man, a woman, and the Lord. It is sacred and beautiful, and it pleases the Lord. He has given us the gift of marriage. The scary thing is, people (even Christians) forget that it is a gift. People complain about their spouse, who is a gift from God. Divorces are so frequent and it grieves the Lord. He designed marriage to be forever. People forget that marriage is a commitment to not only your spouse, but also to the Lord. Make it work, for better or for worse. Love is a choice and too many people forget to choose it when they are irritated or hurt by someone.

After I got engaged, my fiance and I made a commitment to each other that within our marriage the word divorce wasn't going to be in our vocabulary. It is not a thought or a threat to be used to get what we want from our spouse. After we got married, we revisited the conversation and restated that it was not going to be an option. Divorce was off the table and that was final. Our relationship is rooted in the Lord, so anything that comes up can be addressed and moved on from.

Stay committed to your spouse. Stay loyal. Don't speak negatively about them or over them. Trust that the Lord will lead you together for a purpose in times of difficulty and know that He will see you through. Pray for your spouse. Pray for your relationship. The Word says, "Death and life are in the power of the tongue..." (Proverbs 18:21 NKJV). Speak life over each other and over your relationship. Never let someone else's negative speech inspire your negative feelings toward your spouse. Love like Jesus.

In It, But Not Of It

*" I do not pray that You should take them out of the world,
but that You should keep them from the evil one. They
are not of the world, just as I am not of the world.
Sanctify them by Your truth. Your word is truth.
As You sent Me into the world, I also have sent them
into the world."*
John 17:15-18 NKJV

If you continue reading this chapter, you see that Jesus is the One praying and it is for us too, not just those that were with Him.

Friendships can be hard to navigate. When I was little, I had many friends... This wasn't always in my best interest, considering I quickly picked up verbiage, actions, and attitudes of the people I was with. This could have a positive or negative effect. In my experience, it was negative. I am now very thankful for my parents cutting off friendships I didn't know I needed to let go of for a season, to adjust my behavior. As a child, I didn't realize I was shifting because of the people around me, but my parents noticed.

This same principle applies to us as adults or teenagers. We will become like the environment we surround ourselves with. A speaker named Jim Rohn says that we become the average of the five closest people in our lives (Peek, 2024). Who are your five closest people? Who is getting all of your time? Is Jesus one of those five? This is why it is important to surround yourselves with Christian community. Spend the most time with those who will push you to become more like Christ.

How do we witness to unbelievers and fulfill the calling in Matthew 28:19-20 to make disciples if we are only with Christian people? I'm glad you asked! The scripture for today's devotion says, "As You sent Me into the world, I also sent them into the world." We are called to be in the world and bring light to it. Having Christian community is not isolation to that group, it is to strengthen us as we grow in the Lord and support us as we share the gospel of Christ to others. We have to surround ourselves with unbelievers to be able to share Jesus with them. That is why we must be in the world. But, we can not be of the world (or take on the characteristics of the world). The people of the world cannot be your closest circle, but they must be a part of your life.

Allow yourself to be exposed to things of the world in order to bring light, but do not take part in those things. Invite a coworker to dinner, have coffee with an unbelieving friend, say "Jesus loves you" to your cashier at the store. Remember God is your strength, and He will help you not fall to sin when you are exposed to it. He has not placed a calling on your life that He will not equip you for (Hebrews 13:21). "Do not copy the behavior and customs of the world, but let God transform you into a new person by changing the way you think..." (Romans 12:2 NLT).

But, They Hurt Me

"*and forgive us our sins, as we forgive those who sin against us. And lead us not into temptation, but rescue us from the evil one. If you forgive those who sin against you, your heavenly Father will forgive you. But if you refuse to forgive others, your Father will not forgive your sins.*"
Matthew 6:12-15 NLT

In Jesus' earthly ministry, we see time and time again a calling for forgiveness. The scripture above is just one example. It is also listed in later parts of the New Testament. All of scripture is important, but when things are repeated we must pay close attention. The Lord didn't forget that He already put it in the Bible, He wants to drive His point home in our hearts. If we missed it earlier, we will be reminded again later. It is too important to be forgotten or overlooked.

Unforgiveness is something that people too often struggle with. I am guilty of holding onto unforgiveness. I would be bold enough to say that most, if not all, people struggle with it at some point in their lives. Maybe you have been hurt by someone, so have I, and so was Jesus! He was beaten, spit on, mocked, yet He still loved. He did not hold grudges against them. Jesus died for the people that mocked Him as much as He did for the disciples.

I know it is hard to let go of hurt, especially when it comes from someone close to you or someone in the church. I have been there too! We are called to forgive, and the Word says we must forgive others so that we may be forgiven by God. Ask the Lord to help you. He will guide you to the path of forgiveness and grace towards the one who hurt you. Holding onto a grudge is only holding you in bondage. Thoughts of when they hurt you replay in your mind. It is the enemy trying to keep you angry or hurt by them. Ask the Lord to renew your mind, by changing the way you think (Romans 12:2)! Receive freedom from the bondage of unforgiveness by asking the Lord to soften your heart and walk you through the process of forgiveness.

You don't need an apology from that person. Forgiveness is a choice, not a reaction to an apology. People don't always know they have hurt you. You can't sit around and wait for them thinking, "They know what they've done." Guess what? it doesn't matter what they do or don't know; YOU are called to forgiveness. I had to walk through this process with the Lord. It was hard and emotional, but now I have peace when I think about the person who hurt me. I don't know if they meant it or not, but I know I have freedom from bondage. A weight was lifted off of me (I felt physically lighter), when I let go of hurt and walked in forgiveness.

Ask the Lord for help. If you feel like you need to talk to someone, go to another believer you trust and share the hurt and your conviction to begin walking in forgiveness. Ask them to pray for you. There is no shame in needing help. My husband helped me through this process. Allow your heart to be softened and don't let your pride get in the way of the freedom God wants to give you.

Another Seed

"*So we are Christ's ambassadors; God is making his appeal through us. We speak for Christ when we plead, 'Come back to God!'*"
2 Corinthians 5:20 NLT

A fun fact about me is that I danced for eleven years starting when I was about four years old. During my time at dance, I of course learned to dance, but I also learned about ministry. The dance studio I was at was a Christian studio that loved to do outreach and mission work. With that, they often talked about how we treat the people we met during our outreaches. We discussed how we should stand in public to make ourselves look open and kind (not crossing our arms, making sure we smiled, etc.). My instructor always reminded the class that we were Christ's ambassadors. How do we need to act to represent Christ well?

When I was older, and joined the workforce, I had to learn to be firm in my beliefs and realized that more people didn't know the Lord than I thought. The Lord showed me that this was my opportunity to share the gospel with people. I began asking the Lord to use me where He had me to reach the lost. There were many opportunities for me to share my faith with my coworkers and customers.

As I have continued in the public workforce, the Lord has shifted my mindset to keep planting seeds to everyone I can, even if no obvious opportunity comes up. I may be the only Christian they ever meet so I want them to leave thinking something is different about me. I want them to see Jesus in me.

When we meet strangers, even ones that are rude and treat us poorly, we must shift our mindset from "I'll never see them again," to "I'm going to plant seeds and hope I see them again in Heaven." Pray for those who treat you wrong. They do not live according to the standard we have as christians. Approach them with grace and kindness and keep planting seeds.

Dealing with Anxiety

1. *I Trust in God*
2. *Practically Speaking*
3. *It's a Sin*
4. *Sound Mind*
5. *Watch your Words*

I Trust in God

"He holds in His hands the depths of the earth and the mightiest mountains.

The sea belongs to Him, for He made it. His hands formed the dry land, too."

Psalms 95:4-5 NLT

We serve the God who holds the whole world in His hands. How cool is that? He is above all, in control of all, and knows everything that has happened, is happening, and will happen. That is our God! Why are we afraid? Why are we anxious? Fear is an absence of trust in God. Read it again. When I realized this in my own walk through anxiety, I was convicted. How could I not trust the all-knowing One? How could I not trust the One who has always seen me through hard times?

Read Daniel 3. I'll wait... Okay, have we read it? (Insert your "Yes, I have"). Amazing! Shadrach, Meshach, and Abednego refused to serve the false god, even with the threat of being burned alive. In human eyes, they should have been terrified. However, they were confident in the Lord and He sustained them. The Lord was in the fire with them and He did not abandon them. God protected them so much that they didn't even smell like fire.

When we feel anxious, remember we need only to trust in the Lord. He will sustain you. He will not leave you or abandon you. He has you in the palm of His hand. He is your Father (I like to say "my Abba") and He wants to comfort you. Rest in your Father's arms. Trust that whatever you're facing, He already knows the outcome, and He works all things together for the good of those who love Him (Romans 8:28).

Practically Speaking

"Don't worry about anything; instead pray about everything. Tell God what you need, and thank Him for all He has done. Then you will experience God's peace, which exceeds anything we can understand. His peace will guard your hearts and minds as you live in Christ Jesus."
Philippians 4:6-7 NLT

When I first began dealing with anxiety, I didn't really know what to do. I was pretty young when it began and I just remember being scared and running to my parents. They would comfort me, reassure me that everything was okay, and pray for me to have peace. When I was older, I still had anxiety and it actually got worse. I used to not only be generally anxious, but would also randomly have panic attacks (a few a day). But, praise the Lord– He delivered me!

How do you overcome this kind of anxiety? One that seems to never go away. One that feels like it is keeping you from not only your normal tasks, but your God-given dreams and goals. It is just what that scripture says, "pray about everything." We just learned that we must trust in God, but what does that look like practically? It looks like us repeatedly humbling ourselves and going to the Lord for help. Stop thinking you can handle it all on your own, because you can't. Only with God can you overcome it. Tell the Lord what is making you anxious or the topic of your worry and surrender it to Him. Truly learn to let go and let Him take over. Don't hold so tightly to things you can't control, that you don't let the One who can control it help you.

The scripture says that when we pray about it and give gratitude to the Lord, we will experience peace. Give it up and lay everything down at His feet. He wants to give you peace, you just need to come to Him. His Word says when we draw near to Him, He will draw near to us (James 4:8). Draw near to your Father, tell Him what you need, and rest in His peace.

It's a Sin

*"This is my command—be strong and courageous!
Do not be afraid or discouraged. For the Lord your
God is with you wherever you go."
Joshua 1:9 NLT*

What commands do we see in this verse? 1. Be strong and courageous. 2. Do not be afraid. 3. Do not be discouraged. A command means it is an instruction and anything but obedience to that is sin. This means we are commanded to not be afraid nor live in anxiousness and fear is a sin.

Notice I said "live" in fear and anxiety. You can not help if an anxious thought comes to mind, but you do have control over what you do with that thought (2 Corinthians 10:5). You can dwell in that thought and have a lifestyle surrounded by fear and anxiety or you can choose to let go of things you can't control and allow God to step in. You can't help it if getting drunk, lying, or cheating is a temptation. However, we can control our response. We don't do those things because we are commanded not to. You may be tempted to fear, but you must not fall into it. We are commanded not to fear and to trust in God.

A continuation of anxiety or worry happens when we try to control things we can't control. We try to play the role of God and control things we as humans were never meant to handle. Do not let your pride cause you to live tormented by fear when you were created to live in God's peace.

Give it all to the Lord. Don't allow yourself to sin by living in fear. The next part of the verse says that God is with us! Our source of peace and strength is with us everywhere we go! Trust in the Lord and know that He is good, kind, and is all powerful. He is bigger than anything you are afraid of, so let Him show you that side of His character. He desires for you to have that kind of peace and trust in Him.

Sound Mind

"For God has not given us a spirit of fear,
but of power and of love and of a sound mind."
2 Timothy 1:7 NKJV

When I was young and dealt a lot with anxiety, my parents frequently said 2 Timothy 1:7 to me. This verse has helped me through so many anxious temptations. This verse teaches us that fear is a spirit and that it is not from God. The only other source of spirits is the enemy. So, where do you think the spirit of fear comes from? The devil.

How do we deal with spirits that come from the devil to try to harm us (John 10:10)? James 4:7 NLT says, "...Resist the devil, and he will flee from you." We also see during Jesus' earthly ministry He rebuked many evil spirits. Mark 1:25 NKJV says, "But Jesus rebuked him, saying, 'Be quiet, and come out of him!'" This is exactly what we do to remove demonic spirits. We resist the devil by not entertaining the anxious thought and rebuking the spirit of fear and anxiety.

I remember a time when I used to have panic attacks and I began to have one while at a friend's house for Bible study (which, isn't that just like the enemy; trying to distract us from doing the things that please the Lord and strengthen our faith?). I excused myself to the restroom, so as to not make a scene. When I got to the restroom alone, I said out loud (or something along these lines), "Spirit of fear I command you to be quiet and leave in the name of Jesus. I refuse to listen to you anymore. You will not attack me anymore. Be gone in Jesus' name." Key notes from this are speaking out loud (the enemy can give you thoughts be he cannot read your thoughts–only God can), calling the spirit by name (spirit of fear), commanding it to leave (don't ask), and in Jesus' name (we have no power, but Jesus has given us authority through the Holy Spirit). Romans 8:11 tells us that we have the same spirit in us that raised Jesus from the dead. By the power of the Holy Spirit, you are able to conquer the enemy and his demons. Nothing is greater than the power of our God.

Watch your Words

"D*eath and life are in the power of the tongue,
And those who love it will eat its fruit."*
Proverbs 18:21 NKJV

I often hear people who struggle with anxiety say, "I'm just an anxious person," "I have really bad anxiety," or "I've been diagnosed with anxiety." Here is the hard truth: you are going to give yourself anxiety by stating it as a fact about yourself or holding to it as a diagnosis. I do think people can have legitimate issues with chemical imbalances and I do understand that. However, we serve a God who is more than able to heal you from those wounds. You do not have to stay bound to something just because of a diagnosis. I have been in several Bible studies and NO ONE in the church has called this out when people say they are struggling with anxiety. I am not saying it should be called out harshly, but kindly informing that what we say about our lives can and will impact the reality of our situation.

If you struggle with anxiety, stop speaking anxiety over yourself. If you are seeking help or prayer from a trusted individual, begin using language like, "Lately, I have struggled with fear and anxiety and I would like to pray for this." Make it past tense; never speak it over your present or future. Because we will reap the harvest of our words, sow words that are going to bring you closer to the Father and proclaim deliverance.

If you want to see a real change, don't just stop speaking negative "facts" over yourself. Rather, begin to speak life. Begin saying, "I will have a sound mind in Jesus' name, because that is what my Father has for me," or "I know God's will is for me to have peace because that is a fruit of His Spirit." Do not identify with anything outside of what God's Word says about you. His Word says you will have peace; you are a son or daughter of the Most High; you are taken care of by your Creator; you are loved; you were created for a purpose; and so many more. Your identity is not found in your situation or struggles, it is found in the Lord God Almighty, the Creator of the Universe, your Father, your Rock, and what He says about you–and He says you will have peace in Jesus' name. You are not an anxious person, you are a child of the King and His Spirit will produce the fruit of peace in you in Jesus' name.

Dealing with Depression

Fruit of the Spirit

"*But the Holy Spirit produces this kind of fruit in our lives: love, joy, peace, patience, kindness, goodness, faithfulness, gentleness, and self-control. There is no law against these things!*"
Galatians 5:22-23 NLT

This is a simple one and applies to so many areas of struggle, but the Spirit should be producing this fruit in our lives. We should experience joy as long as we are in the Spirit, because the Spirit doesn't take away our joy as a result of a situation. He is always going to be producing that fruit, if we remain in Him.

Abide in the Spirit and you will see the fruit in your life. No matter your situation, keep saturating yourself with the Word of God and continue to get into the secret place. The Holy Spirit will not fail to produce fruit as long as we are connected to the Vine.

Fighting depression can be so hard, I know, I've been there. You must hold onto the fruit of the Holy Spirit. The Holy Spirit will never leave you, so that means His fruit will never leave you. The only thing that can separate you from the fruit is if you detach yourself from the Vine (John 15). Stay rooted in your Father, and hold on to joy.

Joy vs. Happiness

*"Always be full of joy in the Lord.
I say it again—rejoice!"*
Philippians 4:4 NLT

This one is sort of a part two from yesterday's devotion. I want to share something with you that completely changed my approach to fighting the spirit of depression. Happiness is circumstantial, but joy is eternal. Joy is eternal, because it comes from your Father (Nehemiah 8:10). I may not feel happy right now, but I can still choose to have joy and to operate in that fruit.

The Lord taught me this so beautifully. I began struggling with depression at the end of 2019 (I was 15 years old), and it really worsened in 2020. During 2019 and the beginning of 2020 (before COVID really hit), I was teaching dance classes to a sweet group of pre-teens and teenagers. I remember feeling unmotivated and not wanting to teach. I felt so upset that my chest physically hurt. However, when I would teach I would operate in joy, because I couldn't let these sweet girls know I was hurting. I remember realizing I felt so much better when I would teach, because I would be so focused on them and choosing joy. In those moments, I chose to put on a smile and be joyful for them. It was a choice, and when I chose it, I felt better.

Then COVID hit... I remember panicking, because I was scared I would never be happy without being able to teach. I told myself that was my only escape and how I was coping with the pain. I remember crying to the Lord for help, because I couldn't understand why I was struggling so much. In my season of life, I was very blessed and had so many things going well, but I was still hurting inside. It progressed and I eventually dealt with thoughts of suicide. I am thankful the Lord opened my eyes to see that it was the enemy trying to "steal, and to kill, and to destroy;" just like the scripture says in John 10:10, NKJV. I thought to myself, this isn't what I want to do, but I feel tempted to do this. The Lord was my strength through this season and I am grateful He protected me from making any attempt to follow through with those temptations. Eventually, I told my parents, and they were so loving and such spiritual leaders for me to help me walk out of that season in my life.

Through conversations with my parents, and my mom showing me how she worked through postpartum depression, the Lord used her to remind me that joy is a choice. Happiness is fleeting and will only leave us dry. When we choose to operate in the fruit of joy, it will never leave. If you want to see breakthrough and transformation in your life, you must know the difference between joy and happiness.

I have tears on my face as I am writing this, because I know the power of understanding joy will never leave, because the Holy Spirit will never leave. Keep fighting! Don't believe the lies that you aren't good enough (because you are equipped by your Creator to do every good work [2 Timothy 3:17]), that you aren't loved (because your Father in heaven sent His Son to die for you just so He could have a relationship with you [John 3:16]), or that you don't have a purpose (because your Creator created you with a plan and purpose in mind [Ephesians 2:10]).

You always have the Holy Spirit with you, so you always have joy. Keep choosing joy! Keep fighting for breakthrough. The Lord is your strength and even though the season seems to never end now, you will look back and see the Lord's faithfulness on the other side. You are loved. You are cherished. You have a purpose. Friends, keep walking in the Spirit and choosing joy!

Gratitude

" R ejoice always, pray without ceasing, in everything
give thanks; for this is the will of God in Christ Jesus for you.
Do not quench the Spirit... Hold fast to what is good."
1 Thessalonians 5:16-19, 21 NKJV

During the season that I was walking through, I learned that gratitude and despair cannot coexist. It really is that simple! If you are feeling depressed (or maybe you're just kinda sad or having a bad day... it happens), you are not in a state of gratitude. However, God's Word says to give thanks in all things! This isn't just when we feel like it or want to, but in every circumstance be grateful!

I think practically this can look like praying in a place of gratitude more frequently, starting a gratitude journal, or making a habit of saying out loud 3-5 things you are grateful for at the start of every day. For me, a journal never worked... I just wouldn't keep up with it. Praying in gratitude and beginning the day with 3 things I was grateful for were more achievable for me.

When you begin your day with a mindset of gratitude, it changes the course of your day. You are no longer dreading the day to come, but rejoicing and are thankful for another day to be in love with Jesus! Don't just let this be a morning thing, but continue throughout your day with this mindset. It can be easy when you're walking in a season like this, one of grief, or just having a bad day to want to be alone and sit in your feelings. However, isolation is not biblical and we are called to be grateful and have community. Being alone is not the solution to your pain. In fact, it will only make you feel like no one is willing to walk with you through it. The enemy uses isolation to make you feel alone and hopeless. Don't let him win.

Instead of dwelling on your issues, think on things of the Lord! Change your mindset to one of gratitude. Romans 12:2 says, be transformed by the renewing of your mind! Philippians 4:8 says, "...Fix your thoughts on what is true, and honorable, and right, and pure, and lovely, and admirable. Think about things that are excellent and worthy of praise" (NLT). Shift your focus! What are things in your life that you can be grateful for? Start now!

Worship is a Weapon

"*B*ut at midnight Paul and Silas were praying and
singing hymns to God, and the prisoners were listening
to them. Suddenly there was a great earthquake,
so that the foundations of the prison were shaken; and
immediately all the doors were opened and everyone's
chains were loosed."
Acts 16:25-26 NKJV

I just love this story! What an incredible testament to the Lord's
faithfulness and response to our worship and prayer! What can we
take away from these verses? That worship is a weapon against spiritual warfare. No matter what prison we are in and the chains that
are holding us back, worship is how we fight! Worship leads to breakthrough from bondage!

Isaiah 61:3 NKJV says, "...To give them beauty for ashes, The oil of
joy for mourning, The garment of praise for the spirit of heaviness..."
You have been given praise instead of heaviness! It's not just a gift you
have, but it is a "garment!" You are clothed in praise! It is all- encom-
passing! When you praise, your Father takes away the spirit of heaviness. You have a beautiful exchange with the Almighty.

Are you stressed? Are you anxious? Are you depressed? Cast off
the spirit of heaviness and give praise to the Lord! Worship can break
down the walls you have built that are keeping you from the joy and
peace that God has for you. It is time to stop moping in your situation and start praising through it! Stop focusing on yourself and start

focusing on your Father. He's the only one with the power to see you through. Praise Him before the breakthrough, because He is good even if you don't see Him moving right now. Praise Him, because you are alive today and every breath you have is given from Him. Praise Him, because He has led you this far. Praise Him, because He is God!

Taking Control

"For the weapons of our warfare are not of the flesh but have divine power to destroy strongholds. We destroy arguments and every lofty opinion raised against the knowledge of God, and take every thought captive to obey Christ,"
2 Corinthians 10:4-5 ESV

Children let their minds run wild! They use their imagination to think up stories and scenarios that aren't real and use it for play. However, even now as adults or teenagers, it is still easy to let our minds wander. It is easy to let our thoughts run wild with what-if questions... "What if they don't like me?" What if they leave me?" "What if we aren't as close as I thought?" "What if they don't love me or I'm not lovable?" Here lies a big issue! None of these thoughts are biblical.

Take your thoughts and make them obedient to Christ. It is often easier to process this by changing the sentence from "what if" to "even if." Let's make these thoughts obedient to the Word of God. "Even if they don't like me, my Father in heaven is the only One I am trying to please." "Even if they leave me, I know my Father will never leave me." "Even if we aren't as close as I thought, God sent His Son so we could have a relationship." "Even if they don't love me back, I know I am called to love even my enemies and there's nothing that can separate me from God's love."

We must learn to realize when our thoughts are not from the Lord and are becoming disobedient to what His Word says. Pay attention to your every thought and ask yourself if it is aligned with the Word of God. If it isn't, let it go and remind yourself of the truth of His Word. Remember, you aren't alone and your Father is your strength and wisdom to navigate the spiritual warfare at hand. It is time to take control and win the battle in your mind!

Speak Joy

"When I discovered your words, I devoured them.
They are my joy and my heart's delight, for I bear your name,
O Lord God of Heaven's Armies."
Jeremiah 15:16 NLT

Right after I told my parents that I was struggling with depression, they came to me and talked to me about my mom's journey through postpartum depression. The best piece of advice I was given was to have the Word of God on hand at every moment. My mom made flashcards for me with different scriptures written on them. The scriptures were not just random verses, but ones that spoke directly to the situation I was facing. If I was feeling anxious, the verse could say, "Fear not" (Isaiah 41:10 NKJV). If I was struggling with depression, "Count it all joy" (James 1:2 NKJV). If I was struggling with thoughts of suicide, "have life and have it abundantly" (John 10:10 ESV).

Hebrews 4:12 says, "For the word of God is alive and powerful. It is sharper than the sharpest two-edged sword, cutting between soul and spirit, between joint and marrow. It exposes our innermost thoughts and desires" (NLT). In Ephesians 6, we read about the full armor of God. Verse 17 says, "...and take the sword of the Spirit, which is the word of God" (NLT). God's Word is the only offensive part of our armor. His Word is alive and a sword! His Word will win the fight against depression. His Word will win the fight against anxiety. Take up your sword (your Bible) and fight the spiritual battle at hand.

I want to encourage you to make flashcards of your own. Keep them in your purse, bookbag, or pocket. When you feel an attack on your God-given joy or peace, read your flashcards out loud. Remind yourself, and the devil, of God's word. When Jesus was fasting and being tempted by Satan in the wilderness, He fought him by quoting scripture. This is our example. Stand firm on the Word! When you are in a wilderness season, keep speaking scripture out loud. God's Word is powerful and is greater than your trial.

Concluding

1. *Don't Give Up*
2. *God is our Source*

Don't Give Up

"We can rejoice, too, when we run into problems and trials, for we know that they help us develop endurance. And endurance develops strength of character, and character strengthens our confident hope of salvation. And this hope will not lead to disappointment. For we know how dearly God loves us, because he has given us the Holy Spirit to fill our hearts with his love."
Romans 5:3-5 NLT

Not every stage of your walk with the Lord is going to be easy. You won't always feel motivated to read the Bible, to sit in silence and wait for God to speak, or to go to church and be in community. There are days I would've much rather slept in than woken up early and spent my first moments with the Lord, but I know I'm called to discipline. We do not have to be motivated to be disciplined. Discipline is based on habits created to fulfill a need, and motivation is just wanting to do the things we need to do. You don't have to want to do the things you need to do, but you do have to do them anyway. I have noticed that the more time I spend with God the more excited I am to spend time with Him again. Our disciplines become enjoyable the more we do them, especially when those disciplines are bringing us closer to God.

No matter what, keep pushing forward. Even if it's hard or you're tired, remember you serve a God who is far more important than the amount of sleep you get, your work, your school, or your morning coffee. Prioritize Him first, and never let your lack of wanting to make time for God hinder your growth in your relationship with Him.

Your faith and relationship with your heavenly Father isn't something you can focus much attention on for a little while and then you're set. You must keep prioritizing it, over and over again. It is not something you do for a season; it is a life-long priority. So keep choosing Him. Don't quit! He will give you the strength to keep going. Never give up and trust your Father enough to know it will be worth the difficulties.

God is our Source

"*Even though the fig trees have no blossoms,*
and there are no grapes on the vines; even though
the olive crop fails, and the fields lie empty and
barren; even though the flocks die in the fields,
and the cattle barns are empty, yet I will rejoice in
the Lord! I will be joyful in the God of my salvation!
The Sovereign Lord is my strength! He makes me as
surefooted as a deer, able to tread upon the heights..."
Habakkuk 3:17-19 NLT

We have definitely gone over this throughout the book, but it is so important to remember to rest in the Lord and rejoice in His faithfulness. No matter what your situation looks like, God is your joy and strength to endure it to the end. He is the only One who can fill us with what we need to have endurance.

God is the source of our joy, love, strength, kindness, rest, gentleness, hope, peace, patience, endurance, and many more attributes than could ever be listed. He is the only One capable of upholding you, so you make it through. He is your source. Stay connected to Him. Don't leave Him, for He will never leave you.

If you are looking to fill a need in your life, stop looking to the world or to yourself. The world will never be enough, and you will never be enough on your own. Your calling is higher than anything you can do in your own strength. You must seek the Lord to fill those areas. He can give you everything you need to walk the way He has called you to walk. It's time to trust Him!

Sources

Holy Bible, English Standard Version. (2001). Crossway Bibles. (Original work published 2001)

Holy Bible, New King James Version. (1982). Thomas Nelson.

Holy Bible, New Living Translation. (2015). Tyndale House Publishers. (Original work published 1996)

Peek, S. (2024, October 16). *10 principles of success: Quotes to inspire from Jim Rohn.* Business.com. https://www.business.com/articles/10-principles-of-success-quotes-to-inspire-from-jim-rohn/

About the Author

Hi! My name is Ashton Remole. I am 20 years old and married to a wonderful, hard-working, man of God named Stephen. We live in North Carolina near most of our family and friends and are currently pursuing the Lord through personal times with God and through serving and fellowshiping with the local body. I am passionate about the education of believers in regards to their understanding of the Lord and His character and what our response to that should be. I love sharing my testimony and what the Lord has shown me about His goodness and faithfulness through the things He allowed me to walk through. I am also passionate about music in worship and hope to be heavily involved in worship ministry. I pray that God uses this book to speak to you and transform your walk with Him for the better!

www.ingramcontent.com/pod-product-compliance
Lightning Source LLC
Chambersburg PA
CBHW071541120626
46550CB00006B/2537